FIRST AID

IN

COMPOSITION

BY

PETER FITZPATRICK, M.A.

AND

THOMAS HAND, M.A.

ROBERT GIBSON & SONS, GLASGOW, LTD
17 Fitzroy Place, Glasgow G3 7SF

ISBN 0 7169 4026 4

TABLE OF CONTENTS

Page

VOCABULARY
Opposites - - - - - - - - - - - 5
Masculines and Feminines - - - - - - 8
Occupations - - - - - - - - - 11
Double Meaning Words - - - - - - - - 14
Adjectives - - - - - - - - - - - 16
Formation of Nouns - - - - - - - - 19
Formation of Adjectives - - - - - - - 20
Word Games - - - - - - - - - - 21
General Vocabulary Exercises - - - - - - 29

PUNCTUATION
Full Stop - - - - - - - - - - - 36
Capital Letters - - - - - - - - - - 36
Question Mark - - - - - - - - - - 38

COMPOSITION
Sentence Construction — Phrases to Sentences - - - - 41
Answering the question WHEN - - - - - - 44
Answering the question WHERE - - - - - - 46
Conjunctions - - - - - - - - - - 48
'Skeleton' Sentences - - - - - - - - 49
Prepositions - - - - - - - - - - 50
The Missing Sentence - - - - - - - - 51
Sentence Sequence - - - - - - - - - 54
Oral Composition - - - - - - - - - 57
Composition through Pictures:
(a) By Filling Blanks - - - - - - - 58
(b) By Answering Questions - - - - - - 62
(c) By Completing the Story - - - - - - 64
(d) By Describing People, etc. - - - - - - 70
Stories to be Completed - - - - - - - 83

NOTE TO THE TEACHER

Every exercise in this book is meant to lead *directly* towards the writing of composition. Ample scope has been left for *free* expression.

While an emphasis is placed on the writing of composition, many of the exercises can, with advantage, *be treated orally*.

It is felt that at this stage the liberal use of pictures materially assists the child to develop and formulate his ideas.

We recommend that the book should not be worked through simply *from beginning to end* but that the two sections, viz., VOCABULARY and COMPOSITION, should be dealt with concurrently.

VOCABULARY

OPPOSITES

Rover is a BIG dog. Scotty is a SMALL dog.
We say that BIG is the *opposite* of SMALL.

The tiger is a WILD animal. This horse is a TAME one.
We say that WILD is the *opposite* of TAME.

Exercise 1

Fill in the blank spaces with the *opposites* of the words in capital letters: —

A. (1) Mr. Jones is very OLD but his grandson, Bobby, is very ....

(2) A sparrow has SHORT legs. A stork has .... ones.

(3) The prince was RICH but the beggar was ....

(4) France is NEAR to us. Australia is .... away.

(5) John swam in DEEP water while Mary paddled
where it was ....

B. (1) The vegetables were CHEAP but the meat was ....
   (2) Jack's knife is SHARP but mine is too .... to be of any use.
   (3) The lion lives where it is HOT, the polar bear where it is ....
   (4) In summer it is LIGHT at six o'clock. In winter it is ....
   (5) This loaf is STALE. Could I have a .... one?

Exercise 2

In each sentence fill the blank space with the *opposite* of the word in capital letters.

A. (1) Jean's case was LIGHT but Dad's trunk was ....
   (2) The sea was STORMY but the lake was ....
   (3) The NOISY children were ordered to be ....
   (4) The wicked witch was UGLY but the fairy queen was ....
   (5) The sums at the beginning are EASY but those at the end are ....

B. (1) Yesterday was DULL but today has been ....
   (2) The old soldier seemed very CHEERFUL while his companion appeared to be ....
   (3) Make sure everything is TIGHT for .... nuts can cause accidents.
   (4) There was no flood danger where the valley was WIDE, only where it was ....
   (5) These black grapes are SWEET but those green ones are ....

Exercise 3

Here is a list of words with their opposites but the list has become mixed up. Pair them off correctly.

tall	bent
singular	sad
below	short
merry	full
straight	above
empty	plural

Exercise 4

Do the same as for Exercise 3.

front	false

6

clean	double
single	back
quick	kind
true	dirty
cruel	slow

After you have correctly paired off the above lists use each pair of words in a sentence of your own making as in Exercises 1 and 2.

Exercise 5

In each sentence fill the blank space with the *opposite* of the word in capital letters.

A. (1) The house was searched from BASEMENT to ....
   (2) Instead of meeting a GIANT as he had expected, Hans was faced by a ....
   (3) Policemen stood at the ENTRANCE while every .... was carefully bolted.
   (4) At the start of the holidays the station was very busy with the ARRIVAL and .... of many extra trains.
   (5) After WAR comes ....

B. (1) The villagers could now look at the DANGER calmly from the .... of the boats.
   (2) The SILENCE was shattered by the .... of breaking glass.
   (3) The blind beggar could be seen sitting on the wall any day from DAWN till ....
   (4) Every MOUNTAIN and .... rang with the pealing of the bells.
   (5) The king said he would punish COWARDICE and reward ....

Exercise 6

Here is a list of words with their opposites but the list has been mixed up. Pair them off correctly.

day	sea
floor	foot
attack	night
land	sorrow
hand	ceiling
joy	defence

7

Exercise 7

Do the same as for Exercise 6.

friend	nonsense
children	play
summer	foe
darkness	winter
sense	adults
work	light

After you have correctly paired off the above lists, use them in sentences of your own making as in Exercise 5.

MASCULINES and FEMININES

BOY
(masculine)

GIRL
(feminine)

When a word refers to a male, that word is *masculine*.
When a word refers to a female, that word is *feminine*.

MAN is masculine.
KING is masculine.
WAITER is masculine.
DUKE is masculine.
HE is masculine.

WOMAN is feminine.
QUEEN is feminine.
WAITRESS is feminine.
DUCHESS is feminine.
SHE is feminine.

The above words are in pairs. Here are some masculine words in one list and some feminine words in another. Write out the lists, putting them into their correct pairs. For example, in Exercise A which follows, you would pair off the words CONDUCTOR and CONDUCTRESS.

A.
conductor	daughter
uncle	lady
son	conductress
gentleman	princess
prince	aunt

B.
nephew	her
father	nun
monk	niece
earl	mother
him	countess

C.
grandfather	hostess
host	sister
youth	wife
brother	maiden
husband	grandmother

Animals and Birds

Do the same in this exercise.

A.
horse	hen
bull	mare
cock	vixen
fox	cow

B.
drake	goose
gander	lioness
tiger	duck
lion	tigress

Exercise

Replace the words in italics by one of the feminine forms from the jumbled list below: —

DUCHESS, HEN, SISTER, LADY, COW, GOOSE, SOW, NUN, ACTRESS, HEROINE

(1) The farmer took great care of his prize *bull*.
(2) A *cock* was pecking for seed in the farmyard.
(3) The *gander* was a fine old bird with beautiful white feathers.
(4) The carriage of the *duke* stood at the gates.
(5) A medal was awarded to the *hero* of the rescue.
(6) Nothing could be heard but the grunting of the *pig*.
(7) Jean's *brother* is very tall.
(8) The heavy doors were opened by a *monk*.
(9) The *lord* looked up at the walls of the castle.
(10) The *actor* received a great many letters.

Exercise

Replace the words in italics by one of the masculine forms from the jumbled list below. Some other words may have to be changed.

KING, NEPHEW, DRAKE, RAM, MAYOR, MASTER, GROOM, WAITER, USHER, MANAGER

(1)   The *duck* was chased round the yard by a dog.
(2)   The new *mayoress* said that she would do her best for the city.
(3)   The *ewe* bleated loudly when she saw the wolf approach.
(4)   The *queen* spoke to her troops before the battle.
(5)   The hotel *manageress* showed her guests to a room facing the sea.
(6)   The *waitress* wiped the plates before she set them on the table.
(7)   The *niece* was left a fortune by her rich uncle.
(8)   The *bride* thanked all her friends for the lovely presents.
(9)   The *usherette* shone her torch to help the lady to her seat.
(10) The *mistress* of the house spoke to her cook about the dinner for next day.

OCCUPATIONS

Exercise 1

Can you name the occupations of the different people in this picture?

Here are a few more exercises on some of the jobs that men and women do to earn a living.

A great number of these occupations end in the letters "ER", e.g. farm*er*, bak*er*, paint*er*. The occupations of the following people all end in "ER". Can you name them?

Exercise 2

A. (1) One who sells meat.
(2) One who sells fish.
(3) One who sells all kinds of foodstuffs.

(4) One who sells jewellery

(5) One who makes things of wood.

B. (1) One who makes or mends pipes, taps, etc.

(2) One who mends roofs.

(3) One who takes photographs.

(4) One who makes or mends clocks and watches.

(5) One who carries luggage for passengers.

C. (1) One who writes news items for a paper.

(2) One who mends shoes and boots.

(3) One who has studied the law.

(4) One who digs for coal.

(5) One who sells fruit.

"OR" is another common ending. Can you name the following occupations ending in "OR"?

Exercise 3

A. (1) One who acts in a play or film.

(2) One who attends the sick or injured.

(3) One who collects fares on a bus.

(4) One who looks after a building such as a school.

(5) One who cuts coats and suits.

B. (1) An artist who works with stone, plaster, etc.

(2) The person in charge of making a film.

(3) The member of a crew who guides a plane or ship.

(4) An entertainer who performs clever tricks with his hands.

(5) He inspects the work of others.

The following occupations end in "IST". Can you name them?

Exercise 4

A. (1) One who cares for the teeth.

(2) One who sells tobacco, cigarettes, etc.

(3) One who types.

(4) One who paints pictures.

(5) One who mixes or sells drugs, medicines, etc.

12

B. (1) One who plays the piano.
   (2) One who plays the organ.
   (3) One who plays the violin.
   (4) One who writes articles for newspapers.
   (5) One who writes novels.

Do the same as in the above exercises for the following occupations which end in "IAN".

Exercise 5

(1) One who is in charge of a library.
(2) One who is skilled in music.
(3) One who cares for the eyes.
(4) One who deals with electricity.
(5) One who performs seemingly impossible tricks.

Can you tell *or* write a sentence to show what kind of work is done by: —

Exercise 6

A.		B.	
(1)	milliner	(1)	astronomer
(2)	usherette	(2)	surgeon
(3)	mechanic	(3)	secretary
(4)	butler	(4)	composer
(5)	architect	(5)	detective

C. (1) judge
   (2) lumberjack
   (3) glazier
   (4) engineer
   (5) locksmith

c

DOUBLE MEANING WORDS

Many words in English have the same *spelling* and the same *sound* but their *meanings* are entirely different. Take, for example, the word WATCH. Here it is in two sentences:

(1) Would you like to WATCH television?
(2) It was three o'clock on Tom's WATCH.

You can easily see that in the first sentence the word WATCH means *look at* and in the second sentence the word WATCH means a *timepiece*. The spelling is the same; the sound is the same *but* the meanings are *different*.

In the following exercise look at each pair of sentences. Can you discover the missing word in each case? Remember — *same* spelling, *same* sound, *different* meanings.

Exercise

A. (1) (a) Do you think she will .... her driving test?
      (b) The mountaineers climbed to the top of the ....
   (2) (a) .... is one of the best wines in the world.
      (b) A band was playing and flags were flying to welcome the ship into ....
   (3) (a) He does his work ....
      (b) She drew water from the ....
   (4) (a) That is a downright ....
      (b) The corporal told us to .... very still.
   (5) (a) Turn .... at the next cross-roads.
      (b) You have no .... to be here.

B. (1) (a) It's warm enough to do without a ....
      (b) The soldiers were told to open ....
   (2) (a) Eskimos hunt the ....
      (b) .... this letter and post it, please.
   (3) (a) We strolled through the ....
      (b) "You can't .... a car here," he said.
   (4) (a) The tame bird ate crumbs from the .... of my hand.
      (b) The leaves of the .... tree rustled in the breeze.

14

(5) (a) The last day of the .... match was shown on television.
(b) The .... is a lively little insect.

C. (1) (a) In the dark he .... his way towards the door.
(b) Most men's hats are made of ....
(2) (a) Mary .... to me as she passed.
(b) There is a .... missing from this wheel.
(3) (a) I had never seen him looking so ....
(b) Remember to .... the road only when it is safe to do so.
(4) (a) We hired a .... to take us to London.
(b) He is a wonderful swimming ....
(5) (a) Put these pears in a ....
(b) The captain was the next to .... for England.

D. (1) (a) The joiner began to .... a hole through the plank.
(b) Personally I find the old general a frightful ....
(2) (a) The judge's face was ....
(b) We stood near the .... of the ship.
(3) (a) "Write down this ....," said the teacher.
(b) The judge passed ...., on the convicted man.
(4) (a) A .... had begun to build its nest there.
(b) I found it hard to .... the medicine.
(5) (a) The thief .... a large sum of money.
(b) She wore an expensive mink ....

DESCRIBING WORDS OR ADJECTIVES

A squirrel was sitting on a branch of the pine.

A *little red* squirrel was sitting on a branch of the *tall* pine.

The second sentence is more interesting than the first because we have used words which describe the squirrel and the tree. We know now that the squirrel was little and red, and that the pine was tall.

Little, red and *tall* are describing words or adjectives.

Pick out the describing words in these sentences:—

(a) The greedy dog stole a big, juicy bone.

(b) The old castle stood on a steep, rocky hill.

(c) The poor tramp thanked the kind old lady.

Describing words or adjectives do not always come before the words they describe. They can also be used in this way:—

John is *clever.*   That is *correct.*   Mary is not *lazy.*

Mr. Smith is growing *old.*   The weather is becoming *warm.*

Describing words make what we are saying or what we are writing much more interesting. Here are several exercises to help you use them.

Exercise A

Below are printed lists of describing words and beside them lists of persons. Pair off each describing word with the person it suits best.

1		2	
brave	child	kind	leader
poor	driver	funny	acrobat
little	soldier	great	servant
careful	giant	daring	nurse
huge	beggar	humble	clown

Write down sentences of your own, using one pair of the above words in each: e.g., The *brave soldier* now faced the enemy alone.

Now pair off the describing words in the first list with the animals in the second:—

	3		4
cunning	tiger	ferocious	elephant
fierce	chimpanzee	stubborn	mouse
faithful	fox	playful	mule
gentle	dog	lumbering	lion
clever	lamb	tiny	kitten

Use the above pairs in sentences of your own.

Now do the same for these things: —

	5		6
tasty	day	sturdy	scarecrow
comfortable	film	interesting	oak
exciting	meal	daily	bend
rainy	carpet	ragged	book
thick	chair	dangerous	paper

Use the above pairs in sentences of your own.

	7		8
long	garden	nourishing	music
warm	voyage	royal	food
neat	overcoat	electric	traffic
juicy	flower	busy	crown
fragrant	orange	sweet	fire

Use the above pairs in sentences of your own.

Exercise B

Use a suitable adjective to fill the blanks in the following sentences: —

(1) The .... man lifted the front of the car out of the ditch.

(2) A rope-ladder was used to scale the .... wall.

(3) Their voices echoed in the .... room.

(4) Not a sign of life could be seen in the .... desert.

(5) The .... warriors gathered round their chief.

(6) The girl guides made .... preparations for camping.

(7) The .... whale opened its mouth and swallowed the raft.

17

(8) Cattle were grazing in the .... meadow.
(9) The .... fireman rescued the little girl from the blaze.
(10) The citizens were loyal to the .... ruler.

Exercise C

Use these describing words to fill the blank spaces in the little story which follows:—

NEW, GREEN, BUSY, SHORT, DELIGHTED, LOVELY, GOOD, TALL, HUNGRY, WONDERFUL, QUIET

John was .... with his .... bicycle and, as soon as breakfast was over, he set out. His street was not a .... one and soon he was pedalling through the .... countryside. He passed woods of .... pines and .... meadows where cattle grazed. Before turning back, he stopped for a .... rest at Rilby, a .... village five miles from home.

"That was a .... trip," he said to his mother when he returned. "Oh, but I'm ....! I hope there's something .... to eat."

Exercise D

Choose describing words of your own to fill in the spaces in this little story. Try to use a different word each time.

A Day at the Circus

I remember clearly my .... visit to the circus. I liked the clowns best. They were so .... in their .... costumes. The ponies were very ...., too. I was .... at how well they obeyed their mistress's commands. I was rather .... when the lions were brought on. The tamer must have been a very .... man to go into the cage and face such .... beasts. Lastly came the trapeze artistes, ... men and women who performed their act high above the arena. Even a .... mistake would have meant a very .... fall. No wonder the spectators were so ....

18

FORMATION OF NOUNS

In the following exercises form the missing words from the words in capitals in front of each sentence. Here is an example to help you: —

AMUSE.   Snakes and ladders can give us much *amusement* on rainy days.

Exercise 1

A. (1) INFORM   I was given the .... I needed.
   (2) STUDY   James is a new .... at the college.
   (3) DARK   The .... frightened the child.
   (4) AGREE   The statesmen finally reached ....
   (5) NOTE   The .... was pinned up on the board.

B. (1) ASSIST   The shop .... gave me my change.
   (2) APPEAR   I was shocked at his ....
   (3) SILENT   In the desert there was utter ....
   (4) WASTE   Please try to avoid ....
   (5) MEMBER   He applied for .... of the tennis club.

C. (1) SAFE   The rabbit scurried to the .... of its burrow.
   (2) ARRIVE   I haven't seen him since his ....
   (3) MOIST   Plants need ....
   (4) FREE   .... is worth fighting for.
   (5) SCARCE   There is a .... of food in many countries.

FORMATION OF ADJECTIVES

Do the same as in the previous exercise. Here is an example to help you: —

ACT.   These kittens are very *active* little animals.

Exercise 2

A. (1) TRUTH   She is a very .... child.
   (2) ENJOY   The play was most ....
   (3) TERROR   They were in .... danger.
   (4) STORM   The weather remained .... all day.
   (5) ACCIDENT   The crash was purely ....

B. (1) ASTONISH   That is .... news.
   (2) FRIEND   He spoke to me in a .... voice.
   (3) STATION   The vehicle was ....
   (4) BOY   The old man was still fond of playing .... tricks.
   (5) OBEY   His dog is well-trained and ....

C. (1) MOTION   The tiger crouched .... in the grass.
   (2) OAK   The ceiling was supported by thick .... beams.
   (3) PLEASE   We had a .... journey.
   (4) GLORY   It was a .... victory.
   (5) HERO   That was a very .... action.

WORD GAMES

The following exercises (or games) resemble crossword puzzles and could be done on the blackboard with everyone in the class taking part. As well as giving fun, they should provide many new and interesting words. When all the clues have been solved, the initial letters of the answers spell out the names of countries, animals, etc. Here is an example to help you.

	Clue
.. .. s	The opposite of question (6)
.. a .. t	A bit (4)
.. o	A flower (4)
.. n	Not outside (6)
.. .. e	Does not cost much (5)
.. .. l	A night bird (3)
.. .. .. e	A clock keeps this (4)

Some letters have been given to help you. The number in brackets after each clue tells you how many letters there are in the words you have to find. Now here are the answers.

Answer
Part
Rose
Inside
Cheap
Owl
Time

The initial letters of the above words spell out the word APRICOT.

When you have found all the words in the following exercises, use each of them in a sentence of your own.

COUNTRIES

(1) .. .. k   Used in writing (3)

.. .. n .. .. s   Tent material (6)

e .. .. p .. .. .. t   Largest four-footed animal (8)

.. .. s .. o   Used by cowboys for rounding up cattle (5)

.. i ..   We breathe it (3)

n .. .. g .. t ..   Badly behaved (7)

.. .. f f l   Spring flower (8)

(2) m .. .. .. r ..   Up-to-date (6)

.. .. s ..   Not difficult (4)

.. .. .. s   Short for Christmas (4)

.. .. l ..   Unemployed (4)

.. o .. ..   Common fuel (4)

.. d ..   Unusual (3)

(3) n .. v .. .. a .. .. ..   One who guides a ship or plane (9)

.. .. l .. ..   Eskimo's house (5)

g .. .. d .. ..   Masculine of goose (6)

.. y r .. ..   Eagle's nest (5)

.. .. ..   Uncooked (3)

.. .. ..   Unwell (3)

.. g .. .. y   Severe pain (5)

(4) .. .. r ..   They reach a verdict in court (4)

.. l .. ..   High mountains in Europe (4)

p .. .. l .. ..   Not private (6)

a .. t .. f .. c l   Not natural (10)

.. e .. .. ..   Birds build them (5)

(5) .. .. g .. ..   Commence (5)

r .. .. .. o ..   Price paid to free a prisoner (6)

.. t c   Room at the top of a house (5)

.. .. b .. ..   Animal with black and white stripes (5)

.. t .. ..   Makes you want to scratch (4)

.. .. n ..   Narrow road (4)

(6) i .. .. t .. .. ..   First letter of one's name (7)
.. p .. .. e ..   Parts of a bicycle wheel (6)
.. .. c .. u .. ..   A new, untrained soldier (7)
a .. .. i .. ..   To give help (6)
.. l .. c ..   Choose by voting (5)
.. .. .. t .. .. n   A type of lamp (7)

(7) t .. .. r   Soft or delicate (6)
.. n .. l .. m .. .. b .. .. Easily set on fire (11)
b .. i .. ..   Short and to the point (5)
e .. q .. .. .. e   Ask a question (7)
.. .. m p .. .. ..   Storm (7)

(8) .. i o .. .. e ..   One who explores new ground (7)
e e .. .. ..   Weird, sinister, frightening (5)
.. .. p .. d .. ..   Quickly (7)
u .. .. .. e   Join together (5)

ANIMALS

(9) r .. j .. ..   Indian ruler (5)
.. .. .. p .. .. ..   Spear for killing whales (7)
.. .. n ..   Land surrounded by water (6)
.. o .. .. d ..   Wandering herdsmen (6)
.. .. t .. p .. ..   Eight-armed sea creature (7)
c .. .. y   One hundred years (7)
.. n .. .. l .. p ..   Letter holder (8)
r .. .. k .. ..   Takes you into space (6)
.. b .. t .. n .. .. e   As a mule (9)
s .. o .. p .. .. n   Stinging insect (8)

(10) .. e .. .. b .. e   Easily read (7)
e m .. g .. ..   To leave one's country forever (8)
.. p .. o .. t .. n .. t .. A chance (11)
.. .. i .. .. ..   A king's son (6)
.. w .. .. d   Payment or prize (5)
.. .. .. k .. ..   A din (6)
d .. s .. ..   Pudding (7)

(11) k .. .. g .. .. .. h e ..	Riverside bird (10)
.. .. c ... n ..	Very old (7)
.. .. v	A long story (5)
.. .. n l	Army leader (7)
.. n .. .. .. c c	Where the South Pole is (9)
r .. ... b	Aimless walk (6)
.. .. t c .. s ..	Unwanted person (7)
o r .. .. n .. .. y	Not unusual (8)

BIRDS

(12) o .. b	Curved course of a planet (5)
.. .. h .. l	A pupil (7)
.. a .. .. .. w	Used to make candles and soap (6)
r .. .. k .. .. .. w	Far Eastern carriage (8)
.. n .. .. c .. .. t	Not guilty (8)
.. .. .. h .. d	Important church (9)
.. y	Sung in above (4)

(13) .. o .. .. h	To cook or steal (5)
.. x .. .. u .. .. .. n	A lawful killing (9)
l .. .. .. e ..	Ornament for the neck (6)
.. g .. .. r .. .. t	Lacking knowledge (8)
.. h .. r	Tasks in the home (6)
a .. s	A passageway (5)
.. .. .. v .. .. s	Easily excited (7)

(14) p .. .. .. r .. i ..	Painting of a person (8)
.. v .. .. g	Between day and night (7)
n .. t l	Not artificial (7)
.. .. g .. .. t .. c	Huge or enormous (8)
.. s l	Opposite of odd (5)
.. n .. c r .. b ..	Carve letters on stone, etc. (8)
.. u .. s .. r ..	A type of rhyme (7)

FURNITURE

(15) .. .. v .. r .. .. g ..   A king or a coin (9)
     .. m .. .. s .. .. .. l ..   Cannot be done (10)
     d .. e .. .. ..   Dull or dismal (6)
     .. v .. p .. .. .. t .. .. .. Changing water into steam (11)
     b .. .. .. k   Edge of a cliff (5)
     .. .. c h .. .. a   Group of musicians (9)
     .. b .. .. d .. n   To leave, e.g., a sinking ship (7)
     .. .. .. h   Hasty or spots (4)
     .. .. r .. .. g   Bold (6)

(16) w .. r .. .. ..   Where rabbits live (6)
     .. n .. i .. .. p c   It kills germs (10)
     .. o b .. ..   A mechanical man (5)
     d .. .. .. d   Terror (5)
     .. .. d .. c u .. .. .. s   Laughable (10)
     l   Shaped like an egg (4)
     .. u .. c .. .. r   A pirate (9)
     .. s .. u .. .. y   Mouth of a river (7)

(17) d .. s .. s .. .. r   A tragedy (8)
     .. n s .. l .. .. ..   Insulting in manner (8)
     v .. .. .. b .. ..   Can be seen (7)
     .. .. t .. .. t .. o ..   You pay this to your teacher (9)
     .. .. o .. ..   Loop in a rope (5)

FOOD

(18) .. .. n q .. .. ..   Feast (7)
      .. m .. .. n .. ..   Vast (7)
      .. t .. t .. o .. .. r ..   Not in motion (10)
      .. .. r .. .. l .. .. ·   Shaped like a circle
      .. r g .. .. ..   Requiring speedy action (6)
      i .. p .. .. i .. .. t   Annoyed at delay (9)
      .. .. d   Very easily frightened (5)

(19) h .. b .. .. n .. .. ..   To go to sleep for the winter (9)
      .. d .. .. ..   A smell (5)
      .. .. u .. .. ..   Neither masculine nor feminine (6)
      .. x .. l .. .. .. r   One who finds out about a country by travelling through it (8)
      .. .. l ..   Part of an egg (4)

(20) m .. g .. .. t .. .. ..   Seasonal movement of birds, etc. (9)
      .. s s .. u .. ..   Attack (7)
      r .. .. s .. .. k   Search thoroughly (7)
      .. .. n .. .. ..   Sixty seconds or very small (6)
      .. .. s ..   One who paints, draws, etc. (6)
      l .. .. t h ..   Detest (6)
      .. l .. .. w   Permit (5)
      d .. l .. c .. .. .. s   Very tasty (9)
      .. n .. r .. .. c ..   Opposite of exit (8)

A NEW WORD GAME

In this game the aim is to change one word into another word in four or five moves. In each move, *one* letter and *one letter only* must be changed and a new word formed by each change. You are not allowed to change a letter more than *once*. Here is an example to help you.

Change LOSE into FIND in four moves.

LOSE
LONE
LINE
FINE
FIND

In the first exercise you will be given clues for the words in between.

(1) Change SAND into PIPE.
     Clues: *(a)* in one's right mind
            (b) part of a window
            (c) type of tree

(2) Change LOOK to RACE.
     Clues: *(a)* type of bird
            (b) large stone
            (c) old instrument of torture

(3) Change TANK to RUST.
     Clues: *(a)* job
            (b) made of ivory
            (c) a baby would eat one

(4) Change SHOE to CLIP.
     Clues: *(a)* where you buy things
            (b) ocean transport
            (c) small piece

(5) Change FIRE to TALL.
     Clues: *(a)* lose energy
            (b) part of a roof
            (c) a story

(6) Change GOLF to PURL.
   Clues: *(a)* large bay
          (b) sea-bird
          (c) drag

(7) Change RIOT to BOAR.
   Clues: *(a)* grows under the soil
          (b) footwear
          (c) small vessel

(8) Change PAPER to CORNS.
   Clues: *(a)* to leap about
          (b) worn over the shoulders
          (c) worries
          (d) centres of fruits

(9) Change START to CHOKE.
   Clues: *(a)* look hard at
          (b) divide out
          (c) beach
          (d) household task

(10) Change BEARD to TRIMS.
   Clues: *(a)* large furry animals
          (b) rips
          (c) groups of players
          (d) old type of public transport

And now do the following without clues to help you:

   (1) FEEL to MALT.
   (2) WOOD to LARK.
   (3) GATE to MILL.
   (4) LAME to TILT.
   (5) CAME to WENT.
   (6) WORM to TUNE.
   (7) HAND to BORE.
   (8) PRICE to THANK.
   (9) BRUSH to CLAMP.
   (10) STAMP to PLUGS.

GENERAL VOCABULARY EXERCISES

Look at the words in CAPITAL LETTERS at the beginning of each of the following exercises. Fill the blank spaces in the stories with these words *using each word only once.*

Exercise 1

TINKER TOM

BRILLIANT, CLEAN, HUBS, OUTSKIRTS, INTERIOR, SPOKES, DECORATED, VISITED

All the children of the village knew Tinker Tom's caravan. They often .... it on summer days where it stood at the edge of a small wood on the .... of the village. It was painted a .... red with a yellow door and windows. The .... of the wheels were green while the .... were gold. The ...., too, was brightly .... and kept spotlessly .... by Tinker Tom's wife.

Exercise 2

PIRATES

HOIST, SECRET, PRISONERS, CREW, SIGHT, TERROR, PLANK, CARGOES, CHASE, PREY

Captain Cutthroat is the leader of a .... of pirates who are the .... of the seven seas and many proud ships have fallen into their hands. Their chief .... are vessels carrying treasure and other rich .... Whenever they .... a sail on the horizon they .... the Jolly Roger and give .... After a fierce fight, which the pirates usually win, they enslave their .... or make them walk the ...., seize the treasure and either burn the captured ship or tow it back with them to their .... hideout.

29

Exercise 3

EASTER EGG

TINKERING, PAINT, PREPARED, MISCHIEF, SMARTLY, BUSTLE, SPLASHED, DELICIOUS, DIFFICULT, RAMSHACKLE

On Easter Sunday morning there was a great deal of .... throughout the house as everyone .... for the Easter picnic. Mummy was packing lots of .... things into the basket while Dad was .... with the old, ... car. My task, and a .... one it was, was to make sure that Joseph kept out of trouble. Only once did I let him out of my sight and that was when I went for lemonade. On my return, Mum told me that, to keep him out of ...., she had allowed him to .... our names on the hard-boiled eggs. At last we arrived at the picnic spot and the eggs were handed out. When I tapped mine .... it burst and the yolk .... over my shoes. Someone had been at his tricks!

Exercise 4

A CLEAN SWEEP

TURNED, MAGIC, WRONG, SNIFFED, RUINED, REALISED, CLEANED, SHRIEK, STREAM, POURING

Mr. and Mrs. Dawson and the twins, Bob and Jean, were about to sit down to dinner when Bob .... the air.

"I smell soot," he said. "It must be the chimney-sweep I saw at old Mrs. Brown's next door. She said she was going to have her chimney ...." With that he reached for some bread.

"Oh, Mum!" he cried. "Black bread!"

Sure enough, the bread, as if by ...., had .... black. So, too, had the plates, the soup, the tablecloth and everyone and everything in the room. Mrs. Dawson let out a .... when she .... that her well-cooked dinner was .... Mr. Dawson stared at the fireplace from which a .... of soot was ....

"Oh, no!" he shouted. "The chimney-sweep is cleaning the .... chimney!"

Exercise 5

GUIDE DOG

WORTH, TRAFFIC, PERFORM, BLIND, MISTRESS, ORDINARY, TRICYCLES, GUIDE, GOLD, CITY, KERB

Rex is a five-year-old Alsatian. He is not, however, an .... dog because he has been specially trained to .... a certain task. He is a .... dog for the blind. His mistress is a lady who had been .... for many years and who can now move about the .... much more freely since Rex has become her "eyes". Guide dogs are given a long training in cities where there is much .... Rex knows that he has to wait at the .... until the road is clear of vehicles before leading his .... across. He is very clever, too, at avoiding such things on the pavement as prams and .... which could injure his mistress. The blind lady has often said that Rex is .... his weight in ....

Exercise 6

TOYLAND

CHARGER, POPPED, TROOPED, OWNER, APPEAR, STRETCHED, SQUEAKY, GUARDED, GREETED, TRAFFIC

After darkness had fallen and the .... of Terry's Toy Shop had gone upstairs to bed, all the little dolls and golliwogs and .... animals stirred and .... Up .... Mr. Jack-in-the-Box and .... all his friends. A bugle sounded in the nearby fort which .... Toyland from Ratland and out .... the tin soldiers led by Colonel Ironsides on his white .... Lights began to .... in the windows of the Queen's palace just as the cars in the tiny streets were set in motion by a .... policeman. Toyland had come to life.

Exercise 7

TRAPPED

PARTED, CAREFULLY, STRAINING, CAUGHT, SNIFFED, CONCEAL, TERRIFIED, APPROACHED, SAVAGE, STAKE

The hunters had finished digging the pit and now .... placed a net inside it. The top of the hole was covered with grass and leaves to .... it and a young goat was tied to a .... as bait for the tiger. The hunters settled down to wait. A few hours later they heard the snapping of twigs as some big animal .... Very soon the bushes .... and a huge tiger stood on the track. It .... the air and then looked straight at the goat which, by this time, was .... at its rope to escape the brute. With a .... roar the great cat charged at the .... animal but before it had gone very far the ground gave way under it and the tiger was .... in the net.

Exercise 8

BARGAIN DAY

BARGAIN, SALE, LAUGHTER, PRICED, JUMBLE, CAUGHT, SIDE.

At the last Boy Scouts .... sale Mrs. Jefferson saw a very good looking spring coat lying on a heap of garments all .... very cheaply. This, indeed, was a .... Mrs. Jefferson hastily slipped out of her new fur coat, laid it on the counter and tried on the coat that had .... her eye. While she was doing this, another lady, thinking that the fur coat was for ...., tried it on and paid for it. When Mrs. Jefferson saw what had happened she was very angry at first but afterwards saw the funny .... of it and joined in the ....

Exercise 9

ADRIFT

DOWNSTREAM, CASTAWAYS, CONSTRUCT, CURRENT, LAUNCHED, OPEN, STEERED, GRADUALLY, CONTROL, IMAGINING

It had taken Jim and Fred two days to .... their raft. When all was ready, the craft was .... and the boys .... themselves across the river by means of long poles. .... themselves pirates or the .... of "Coral Island", they spent a very happy afternoon on the raft. No one noticed that the .... had .... taken them farther and farther .... until suddenly they found that they were unable to .... the speed of the raft. Faster and faster they floated down the river. Terror seized the boys.

"We're heading for the .... sea!" yelled Jim.

Exercise 10

RIDING ON AIR

AIR-FILLED, TRAVELLERS, VEHICLES, NOWADAYS, IDEA, SOLID, PROVED, UNCOMFORTABLY, MANUFACTURERS

In the early days of cycling and motoring .... were fitted with .... rubber tyres. This meant that ...., even on good roads, had a very bumpy ride. It was a man called Dunlop who, after watching his son riding .... on his new bicycle, had the .... of filling tyres with air. The new .... or pneumatic tyres were first fitted on bicycles and .... so successful that motor .... adopted them. .... all road vehicles have these tyres.

Exercise 11

THE COWBOY

LEAN, CHECKED, OCCASIONALLY, VERANDAH, SWEPT, WITHDREW, NOONDAY, PRAIRIE, WIDE-BRIMMED, DESERTED

Tex Campbell lounged on the .... which shaded him from the heat of the .... sun. His .... hat was pulled well over his eyes. It was covered with the grey-brown dust of the .... trails and in its high crown there was a couple of neat round holes. His face was nut-brown and .... and he had not shaved for a week. Alert, grey eyes .... up and down the .... street, resting on the bat-wing doors of the saloon opposite. Idly he .... a Colt from the right-hand holster and .... that it was fully loaded.

Exercise 12

THE "QUEEN MARY"

COMPANY, RESPECTED, CUSTOM, MISTAKEN, REMARKED, DELIGHTED, VESSEL, OTHER, LINER, IMPOSSIBLE, CHOICE

It was the .... of the Cunard Line to end all their ships' names in 'IA' and the latest .... was to be called the "Queen Victoria". While the giant .... was being built, the chairman of the Cunard .... happened to be speaking to King George V and .... that the

33

new Cunarder was to be named after one of Britain's most .... queens.

"Her Majesty *will* be ....!" exclaimed the King before the .... could finish. The chairman found it .... to tell the old King that he was ...., and so there was no .... but to call the ship the "Queen Mary".

Exercise 13

SHOOT!

SELECTED, ONLOOKERS, CLUTCHED, GLARED, DIRECTOR, SIGNAL, COILED, COLLAPSED, APPROACHED

The two men .... at each other in the early morning light. Mist .... like serpents about their ankles. Despite the chill neither man wore a coat or hat. From a knot of .... standing at the side of the field one man ...., carrying a long, flat box in which lay two pistols. He offered the box to the two men who each .... a weapon. Exchanging a final glare they turned and stood back to back. At a given .... they marched ten paces, turned and fired. One man staggered, ...: at his chest and ....

"Cut!" yelled the .... "Let's play that scene again."

Exercise 14

WRECKERS

SURVIVORS, NEXT, DEMOLISHING, STRETCH, BEACONS, LURING, AGROUND, EVIL, EXTINGUISH

Have you ever heard of *wreckers*? They had nothing to do with .... rickety, old buildings but their .... business lay in .... ships to their doom, then murdering the .... and stealing the cargo. Wreckers usually operated on a rocky, dangerous .... of coastline. They would wait for a dark, stormy night and .... the warning beacons on the cliff tops and hope that a ship would run .... Sometimes they lit .... at suitable places inland so that vessels, mistaking their distance from shore would be driven on to dangerous rocks. In .... to no time the wreckers would be at work.

34

Exercise 15

PRESS GANG

SEVERAL, TAVERN, PREVIOUS, UNFORTUNATE, BEFRIEND, METHODS, RECRUITS, ENROLLED, SERVE, SPOTTED

In .... centuries life in the Royal Navy was very hard and so it was difficult to find men to .... in it. The Navy, therefore, filled its ships with .... taken from the jails or with men who were .... enough to meet the *Press Gang.* This gang would be sent ashore from a naval ship at some big port such as Bristol. If they .... a healthy young man drinking in a ...., they would ;........ him and make him drunk. The poor man would then waken up to find himself .... in the Navy for .... years during which time he might not see his family at all. If the press gang happened to be in a hurry, they used rougher ....

PUNCTUATION

THE FULL STOP

(a) A FULL STOP is used to mark the end of a sentence.

Example: The gardener cut the grass with a lawn-mower.

(b) A FULL STOP is used to show that a word has been SHORTENED.

Example: Doctor becomes *Dr.*
Street becomes *St.*

(c) A FULL STOP is used when only initial letters are written instead of the full word.

Example: P.R. Jones
A.D.

Now place the FULL STOPS correctly in this exercise.

Exercise

(1) Mary poured out some milk for her kitten
(2) At the corner of Russell Ave there is a little sweet shop
(3) Mr and Mrs Robertson carefully locked up their house before going off on holiday
(4) The letter was addressed to Sgt D Hawkins of the RAF
(5) At 10 am the wedding guests started to arrive at St Paul's

CAPITAL LETTERS

You have learned that full stops are used to end sentences. You must also remember that CAPITAL LETTERS are used to *begin* sentences.

Example: The runaway horse was stopped by the brave action of a policeman.

Now re-write the following sentences correctly.

Exercise

(1) he sat down in the armchair.
(2) roses bloom in the summer.
(3) a black cat is the sign of good luck.
(4) the children played in the snow.
(5) look before you leap.

Apart from the capital letter at the beginning of a sentence, there are certain words which *must* begin with a capital letter whether they are at the beginning of a sentence or not. Such words are:—

a.   *The names of people:*   John, Mary, Smith, Mr. Campbell, Mrs. Watson, Miss Johnson, Dr. Freeman.

Now write out these names correctly:—

bob, catherine, williams, mr. park, mrs. brown, miss davis, dr. cook.

b.   *The names of towns, counties, countries, rivers, etc.:* London, Hamilton, Kent, Spain, Tweed, North Sea, Pacific Ocean.

Now write out these names correctly:—

dover, edinburgh, devon, canada, nile, irish sea, indian ocean.

Now here is an exercise on the above rules. Before you begin, however, go over with your teacher the rules for FULL STOPS and CAPITAL LETTERS. Remember what they are:—

BEGIN EACH SENTENCE WITH A CAPITAL LETTER AND END IT WITH A FULL STOP.

THE NAMES OF PEOPLE AND PLACES MUST HAVE CAPITAL LETTERS.

FULL STOPS ARE USED TO SHOW THAT WORDS HAVE BEEN SHORTENED.

Re-write the following sentences correctly.

Exercise A

(1) fred is going to paris
(2) he was born in glasgow
(3) we went sailing down the thames

(4)   there is a perth in scotland and a perth in australia
(5)   we crossed the atlantic ocean to new york

Exercise B

(1)   many of these tribesmen live in south africa
(2)   the city of rome stands on the river tiber
(3)   many people in india believe that the ganges is a sacred river
(4)   dr watson and his son, james, have been to egypt
(5)   mr and mrs carter were invited to our house

QUESTION MARK

When you write down a question, you must remember to put a
QUESTION MARK (?) at the end. For example:

> Have you seen him?
> Where are you?
> How did you manage to do that?
> Can she swim?
> Who is this boy?
> When does the concert begin?
> Why was our team beaten?
> What have you been doing?

Exercise

Decide for yourself which of the following are questions, and
write them out, putting a QUESTION MARK at the end.

A. (1)   How is the patient.
    (2)   I don't know the answer.
    (3)   Could you come, too.
    (4)   Why are you leaving early.
    (5)   I suppose that is true.
    (6)   Let me ask you a question.
    (7)   When does this train leave.
    (8)   What is your name.
    (9)   How much is this.
   (10)   How far it is I don't know.

B. (1) Where are you going.
   (2) Tell me your name.
   (3) Can you ride a pony.
   (4) Come with me.
   (5) Give me your reason for this.
   (6) Is this an express train.
   (7) Fasten your safety belts, please.
   (8) You speak English, don't you.
   (9) Who goes there.
   (10) Where have you been.

Here are some little stories, each only two sentences in length, but the FULL STOP and CAPITAL LETTER between the sentences have been left out. Decide for yourself where the first sentence ends and the second sentence begins and then re-write them with the punctuation in its correct place. Here is an example to help you:—

At nine o'clock exactly the doors of the huge store were flung open hundreds of women rushed forward in search of a bargain.

This becomes:—

At nine o'clock exactly the doors of the huge store were flung open. Hundreds of women rushed forward in search of a bargain.

Exercise

A. (1) Jean has a lovely budgerigar she feeds it every day with bird seed.
   (2) A sand-storm is blowing up the tribesmen draw their long robes about their heads and faces.
   (3) The great axe falls for the last time slowly the giant pine begins to topple.
   (4) John played very well in the trial game last week we expect that he will be picked to play in the first match of the season.
   (5) Our leader spread out a huge map we gathered round to listen to his plans.

B. (1) The lights turned from red to red and amber, and from that to green the long line of traffic began to move forward.

   (2) Fred switched on the television set the news was just beginning.

   (3) In no time the workmen had unloaded picks, shovels, hammers and drills from the lorry they fenced off the road and began to dig it up.

   (4) The city was filled with thousands of Christmas shoppers it was almost impossible to move freely among the crowds.

   (5) Jamaica Jim slowly counted forty paces from Hangman's Tree and stopped it was here he should find the buried treasure.

In this section there are *three* sentences in each little story. Decide for yourself where the full stops and capital letters should be.

C. (1) The policeman turned the handles of all the doors in the street they were all locked except one cautiously he pushed it open and stepped inside.

   (2) The Girl Guides and Brownies arrived at the camp site the camping equipment was speedily unloaded from the lorry and everyone set to work soon a spick and span camp had been set up.

   (3) A blizzard howled for four days across the frozen country no living thing was able to go out of doors the people in the village were beginning to worry about their food supply.

   (4) Trains packed with people left for the coast every fifteen minutes the beaches rapidly filled with bathers not even the traffic jams could dampen the joy of the holidays.

   (5) The waiter was carrying two plates of hot soup across the restaurant on his way he tripped over an umbrella the plates flew out of his hands and landed on the lap of a gentleman who was waiting to be served.

COMPOSITION

SENTENCE CONSTRUCTION

PHRASES TO SENTENCES

A group of words which does not make complete sense by itself is called a PHRASE. Here are some phrases: —

(1) on my way to school
(2) at the concert
(3) reading a book
(4) in early spring

You will see that each group of words needs some words added to it to make *complete sense*. When this has been done, we have a sentence. We will now make these four PHRASES into SENTENCES.

(1) *I am* on my way to school.
(2) *Joan sang* at the concert.
(3) *Father is* reading a book.
(4) *Buds begin to appear* in early spring.

These groups of words now make *complete sense* and so we call them sentences. Look at the first word of each sentence. Have you noticed that it begins with a CAPITAL LETTER? When you write sentences, *always* remember to start with a CAPITAL LETTER. Now look at the end of each sentence. You will see a dot called a FULL STOP or PERIOD. When you write a sentence *always* remember to put a FULL STOP or PERIOD at the end.

Exercise

Here are some PHRASES. Could you turn them into SENTENCES by adding a few words to the BEGINNING? Do not forget capitals and full stops.

(1) .... by the fireside
(2) .... through the snow
(3) .... into the water
(4) .... yesterday evening

(5)   .... at school
(6)   .... at the zebra crossing
(7)   .... under the trees
(8)   .... by bus
(9)   .... at daybreak
(10)   .... with my brother and sister

Here are some PHRASES. Turn them into sentences by adding words TO THE END. Here are two examples to guide you:—

(a) on the television ....   *becomes*
       On the television we saw the space-ship take off.

(b) in the harbour ....   *becomes*
       In the harbour lay a fleet of ships.

Now do the same in this exercise.

Exercise

(1)   after breakfast ....
(2)   on the sands ....
(3)   into the circus ring ....
(4)   on the table ....
(5)   with his huge axe ....
(6)   lying on the table ....
(7)   down the river ....
(8)   sitting cross-legged before his tent ....
(9)   into the air ....
(10)   with a roar of rage ....

Exercise

Fill the blank spaces with suitable words or phrases to make complete sentences.

A. (1)   .... are being mended.
    (2)   .... has lost his ball.
    (3)   .... are lying all over the floor
    (4)   .... ran gaily about the meadow.
    (5)   .... is directing the traffic.

42

(6) .... is painting the kitchen.
(7) .... are great friends.
(8) .... played with his blocks.
(9) .... told Billy a bed-tims story.
(10) .... is burning brightly.

B. (1) The soldier .... on guard.
(2) Many boys and girls .... in the street.
(3) The toys .... in Santa's bag.
(4) The clown .... flat on his face.
(5) The goldfish .... round and round in its bowl.
(6) Robin Hood .... the Sheriff's men.
(7) Many flowers .... in the garden.
(8) The children .... at Punch and Judy.
(9) The teacher .... on the blackboard.
(10) The rain .... against the window-pane.

C. (1) The bandits robbed ....
(2) Jack quickly filled ....
(3) The angry bull stamped ....
(4) The old cat finally caught ....
(5) Two dogs were eating ....
(6) The fire soon destroyed ....
(7) A horse was pulling ....
(8) Mother was dusting ....
(9) The candles lit up ....
(10) The flood damaged ....

ANSWERING THE QUESTION "WHEN"

Exercise

Pair off correctly column A with column B.

A.	B.
(1) The cuckoo arrives here	in the autumn.
(2) The harvest is gathered	in the morning.
(3) School begins	in winter.
(4) The milk is delivered	in the spring.
(5) Snow falls	at nine o'clock.

Exercise

Complete the following by adding one or more words to the end of each.

(1) Apples fall from their trees when ....

(2) Our snowman melted when ....

(3) We should visit the dentist whenever ....

(4) The tramp thanked the lady after ....

(5) The little girl smiled as soon as ....

We can sometimes make our sentences more interesting if we make them longer by answering the question WHEN.

e.g. *We went to the sea-side.*

This is a sentence but it tells us very little. Let us make it longer and slightly more interesting by answering the question WHEN.

We went to the sea-side. WHEN?

We went to the sea-side during the summer holidays. The phrase "during the summer holidays" tells us WHEN the trip to the sea-side took place. If you wish you may place this phrase at the beginning of the sentence. Thus,

During the summer holidays *we went to the sea-side.*

Now try the following exercises in the same way.

Exercise

A. (1) Carol singers sang in the streets ....
  (2) The coal merchant delivers coal ....
  (3) .... many ladies wear fur coats.
  (4) John and Anne polish their shoes ....
  (5) .... the young birds will leave the nest.
  (6) We like to go for walks ....
  (7) ...., the garden was a mass of flowers.
  (8) The dentist visits this school ....
  (9) The foolish boy was hit by a motor car ....
  (10) .... Helen found two coins on the pavement.

B. (1) Bullets whistled around his head ....
  (2) No sound could be heard ....
  (3) The fire engines roared through the streets ....
  (4) .... Mother was setting the table for tea.
  (5) .... Joan handed the grocer the money.
  (6) Dick was hit by a flying snowball ....
  (7) .... the twins received many cards and presents.
  (8) Father says he will mend the fuse ....
  (9) .... the boys heard a scream.
  (10) The bus stopped suddenly ....

ANSWERING THE QUESTION "WHERE"

Pair off correctly columns A and B.

A.	B.
(1) The children went skating	in the hearth.
(2) The soldiers marched	before the judge.
(3) A log fire blazed	under a tree.
(4) We sheltered from the rain	on the frozen pond.
(5) The prisoner was brought	through the streets.

Exercise

Complete the following by adding one or more words to the end of each.

(1) The hare raced across ....
(2) The treasure was hidden under ....
(3) The airliner flew over ....
(4) He took his tools from ....
(5) The cottage stood beside ....

Exercise

Fill the blank space in each sentence with a suitable word.

(1) People live in ....
(2) Soldiers live in a ....
(3) Miners work in a ....
(4) We find captured wild animals in a ....
(5) Camels can be seen in the ....
(6) Pet birds live in ....
(7) Pet rabbits live ....
(8) Pupils work in ....
(9) Apples grow on ....
(10) Babies sleep in ....

In the above exercise you completed the sentences by answering the question "WHERE?" Sentences can be made longer and more interesting by adding, where possible, a group of words which answers the question "WHERE?"

e.g. *The tiger lay in wait for its prey.*

We could make this sentence more interesting by answering the question WHERE. Thus,

The tiger lay in wait for its prey by the side of a water-hole.

The phrase "by the side of a water-hole" tells us WHERE the tiger was hiding and makes a better sentence. If you wish you may place this phrase at the beginning of the sentence. Thus,

By the side of a water-hole *the tiger lay in wait for its prey.*

Now try the following exercises in the same way.

Exercise

A. (1)   .... logs were stacked high for winter.
   (2)   A policeman stood directing traffic ....
   (3)   Pigeons ate the crumbs ....
   (4)   The boy held on tightly ....
   (5)   .... the ship struck hidden rocks.
   (6)   .... vultures flew in slow circles.
   (7)   Many children were paddling ....
   (8)   .... a single shot was fired.
   (9)   The secret paper was found ....
  (10)   .... the clowns rolled about madly.

B. (1)   A fire was started ....
   (2)   The prisoners were kept safe ....
   (3)   The policeman caught the thief ....
   (4)   .... a new library was built.
   (5)   .... the smugglers lay hidden.
   (6)   There was a loud explosion ....
   (7)   .... the girls gathered wild flowers.
   (8)   .... the enemy's camp could be plainly seen.
   (9)   A soft breeze blew ....
  (10)   The goat escaped by jumping from rock to rock ....

CONJUNCTIONS

Your compositions can sometimes be made more interesting if you join two or more simple sentences together by using the words AND or BUT. These two words are called *joining words* or CONJUNCTIONS. You must not, of course, use these two words too often. *Once* is usually enough in a sentence. Here are two examples to help you.

(a)　Little Mary said her prayers. She jumped into bed.

This becomes:—

Little Mary said her prayers *and* jumped into bed.

Notice that the word "she" is not needed in the longer sentence.

(b)　A huge fire was burning in the grate. The room was still cold.

This becomes:—

A huge fire was burning in the grate *but* the room was still cold.

Now try the following exercises. Join the two sentences by using a suitable conjunction.

Exercise

A. (1)　The policeman walked slowly along the street. He did not see the thief.

(2)　Every girl should have a ticket. She may pay at the gate.

(3)　Men were mending the road. No traffic was allowed to use it for two days.

(4)　We feel he should be invited to the party. His manners are too bad.

(5)　The soldiers searched the castle. They could not find the spy.

B. (1)　A little man jumped out of the hollow tree. He made signs for me to come closer.

(2)　I approached fully armed. I still felt afraid.

(3)　This is the room where the money was found. Here is the key of the chest.

(4)　A prize is not given to everyone. All must work hard.

(5)　John is a strong boy. He should do well in the school team.

C. (1) The food was running short. More supplies were on the way.
   (2) The guard waved his flag. The train left the station.
   (3) Billy upset the vase. Luckily it did not break.
   (4) It was cup final day. Thousands of people had come to see the game.
   (5) John is good at his work. Fred is even better.

SKELETON SENTENCES

Write sentences using the guide words given in the following exercise. An example is done to help you.

A cow .... grass .... meadow.

This can be made into a sentence. Thus,

A cow was eating grass in the green meadow.

Now try this exercise.

Exercise

A. (1) Father .... fire .... match.
   (2) A goldfish .... swimming .... bowl.
   (3) A giant .... villagers .... castle.
   (4) The king .... troops .... enemy.
   (5) The wind .... leaves .... trees.

B. (1) The playground .... filled .... children .... games.
   (2) A flash .... struck .... toppled .... ground.
   (3) John .... snow .... boots .... wet.
   (4) Alice .... purse .... five .... police.
   (5) Sunlight .... classroom .... pupils .... lessons.

C. (1) Everyone .... afraid .... tiger .... escaped .... cage.
   (2) The crew .... ship .... lifeboats .... fire .... decks.
   (3) .... accident .... doctor .... bandage .... child .... hospital.
   (4) Darkness .... castle .... sentry .... forwards .... night.
   (5) .... Mother .... knitting .... socks .... kitten .... wool.

49

PREPOSITIONS

In the following exercise use the words in capital letters to complete each of the sentences which follow:—

ACROSS, WITH, THROUGH, BETWEEN, ON, BY

(a) We walked .... the wood.
(b) Bring your rucksacks .... you.
(c) I stood .... Jim and Fred.
(d) The vase was .... the table.
(e) The sailors rowed .... the bay.
(f) The book was written .... Scott.

TO, FROM, BENEATH, ABOVE, BESIDE, UPON

(a) Jack hid .... a pile of hay.
(b) Jet 'planes passed .... us
(c) This liner has arrived .... New York.
(d) I am going .... London.
(e) By standing .... my shoulders, he reached the ledge.
(f) The cottage stood .... the lake.

AMONG, PAST, OF, OFF, IN, INTO

(a) The treasure was divided .... the three survivors.
(b) The soldiers marched .... the Governor.
(c) The rest .... you will have to wait.
(d) Four people were .... the room.
(e) Jack came .... the room.
(f) He fell .... his horse.

BEFORE, AFTER, UP, DOWN, FOR, AGAINST

(a) He climbed .... the hill to the top.
(b) The team prepared .... the match.
(c) The traitor plotted .... his king.
(d) He slipped .... the steep mountainside.
(e) .... the battle the wounded were carried from the field.
(f) I have something to tell you .... your departure.

(a)   The ship lay .... the quay.
(b)   You should wash your hands .... a meal.
(c)   The runner raced .... the tape.
(d)   The spy hid .... the heavy curtains.
(e)   I first got to know him .... the war.
(f)   I have not seen her .... last Sunday.

THE MISSING SENTENCE

In the following exercise you are asked to fill in the middle one of three sentences, the first and third being given. Look at the example below. By studying the two given sentences it is not difficult to imagine what the second sentence might be.

Example:
(a)   John turned at the gate and waved good-bye to his mother.
(b)   ....
(c)   He hurried back to fetch it.

Here is one possible way of filling in the missing sentence:—

(b)   He had not gone far when he remembered that he had left his train ticket in his other suit.

There are, of course, other possibilities. For example:—

(b)   She called to him that he had forgotten his packet of sandwiches.

Or

(b)   She held up his raincoat which he had left on the hall-stand.

In this exercise your sentences may be short or they may be quite long, but you should make them as interesting as possible. Remember to read over the three sentences when you have finished to see that, together, they make *complete sense*.

Exercise

A. 1. *(a)* Ruth felt very nervous as she entered the gates of her new school for the first time.

  (b) ....

  (c) After that she felt much happier.

 2. *(a)* One afternoon Bob and Peter were walking home from school.

  (b) ....

  (c) Bob rushed to warn the neighbours while Peter telephoned for the fire brigade.

 3. *(a)* Old Adams lived alone in a big house just outside the

  (b) village.

  (c) ....

  (c) That is why he seldom had a visitor.

 4. *(a)* Larry was a keen stamp collector.

  (b) ....

  (c) He rushed in to buy it.

 5. *(a)* Hastings and the other two leaders reined in their horses at the top of the ridge.

  (b) ....

  (c) Jeffrey rode back to tell the settlers the good news.

B. 1. *(a)* Fred pocketed the tape measure and began to cut the linoleum.

  (b) ....

  (c) He threw up his hands in horror.

 2. *(a)* Tess enjoyed the party.

  (b) ....

  (c) She had to spend three days in bed.

 3. *(a)* We were due to take off at half-past two.

  (b) ....

  (c) Our departure was delayed for three hours.

 4. *(a)* He set off alone at dawn.

  (b) ....

  (c) He was beginning to regret that he had not taken the old guide's advice.

5. 4. *(a)* Bob pedalled furiously down the steep hill.
    (b) ....
    (c) Cut, bruised and wet, he struggled to his feet.

C. 1. *(a)* Swallows leave this country in autumn.
    (b) ....
    (c) They return in spring.
   2. *(a)* The six competitors stood poised on the edge.
    (b) ....
    (c) As they surfaced, Jeff was in the lead.
   3. *(a)* As we marched along, all seemed peaceful enough.
    (b) ....
    (c) We hastily dived for what cover we could find.
   4. *(a)* The summer holidays were still a long way off.
    (b) ....
    (c) They practised saying a few simple phrases in Italian.
   5. *(a)* The rabbit scurried off at the sound of barking.
    (b) ....
    (c) There it felt safe.

D. 1. *(a)* The police car sped across the tarmac.
    (b) ....
    (c) At all costs the 'plane must be prevented from taking off.
   2. *(a)* I will never forget that terrible winter.
    (b) ....
    (c) Helicopters from a nearby airfield kept the village supplied.
   3. *(a)* The school bell rang.
    (b) ....
    (c) They began the first lesson of the day.
   4. *(a)* Mary picked up the "Radio Times."
    (b) ....
    (c) She hurried to the television set and switched on.
   5. *(a)* The old tramp pushed open the gate.
    (b) ....
    (c) Disappointed, he turned away.

SENTENCE SEQUENCE

The following exercises consist of a number of paragraphs. The sentences of these paragraphs, however, are *not* in their correct order. Your task is to re-arrange them correctly by using your common-sense and imagination. When you have read them over carefully, decide what the *first* sentence of the paragraph will be. You will find that the other sentences follow fairly easily after that.

Here is an example to help you:—

(1) His keen eyes can spot a fat, juicy worm from afar off and before the worm knows what has happened, it is being served up to Mrs. Blackbird in the nest.
(2) Father Blackbird is a very clever and bold little bird.
(3) While his wife is hatching the eggs in their snug little nest, he is out searching for food.
(4) After the young Blackbirds have hatched out of their eggs, they are very hungry and Mrs. Blackbird then joines her husband in fetching them worms.

After having carefully read the above sentences most of you will agree that the paragraph, correctly arranged, should read:—

Father Blackbird is a very clever and bold little bird. While his wife is hatching the eggs in their snug little nest, he is out searching for food. His keen eyes can spot a fat, juicy worm from afar off and before the worm knows what has happened, it is being served up to Mrs. Blackbird in the nest. After the young Blackbirds have hatched out of their eggs, they are very hungry and Mrs. Blackbird then joins her husband in fetching them worms.

Now do the following exercises in the same way.

Exercise

A. (1) He could hardly wait till the good weather arrived so that he

54

could sail his yacht in the boat-pond.

(2) Last year Jim received a three-foot yacht for his birthday.

(3) At last Jim's parents took him on holiday to the sea-side where his yacht won first prize in a sailing race.

(4) This was a present he had always wanted.

B. (1) When they arrived, they were very curious to learn all about "Nessie," the strange monster which is supposed to live in the depths of the loch.

(2) No one, however, had ever seen the monster at close range.

(3) Jean and Richard Blair were off to visit their Aunt Margaret who lives in Fort Augustus.

(4) Aunt Margaret told them that several people had claimed to have seen "Nessie" and one or two had even taken photographs of something very odd far out in the loch.

(5) This lovely town is situated on the shores of Loch Ness in Scotland.

C. (1) Alice's mother tended the robin all through the winter until its wing healed.

(2) One day at the end of autumn Alice found an injured robin lying under a hedge.

(3) Carefully the girl lifted the terrified little thing and hurried home with it.

(4) The poor creature had a broken wing and was making vain attempts to fly.

(5) By spring the chirpy little bird had become the family pet and after it was released it kept returning to the window sill each day for titbits.

D. (1) Finally they had to haul Dad away, reminding him that he had spent much more than he said he would.

(2) Sally drove Dad and Jim took Mum.

(3) Dad said that he would give each of them their pocket money and no more.

(4) From then on they visited in turn the Steamboat, the Sky Rocket, the Waltzer, shooting galleries, coconut shies and most of the slot machines.

(5) When Saturday arrived Mum and Dad, as they had promised, took the twins, Sally and Jim to the fairground.

(6) The sound of the music and squeals of laughter made them hasten their steps towards the huge field where the stalls had been set up.

(7) First of all they tried the Dodgem cars.

E. (1) Immediately the superintendent telephoned the police, who warned the people in the neighbourhood to stay indoors.

(2) Near midnight the police received a telephone call from a farmer who said he had trapped the lion in his barn.

(3) All the keepers at the zoo searched the area thoroughly especially the fields where cattle and horses were grazing.

(4) At feeding time in the zoo it was discovered that Kraka, the lion, had escaped.

(5) As soon as Kraka had bounded after the meat, the brave farmer slammed the door.

(6) Seeing the brute prowling round his yard in search of food, he had quickly thrown a large piece of meat into the barn.

F. (1) Unfortunately, he pulled up many young plants as well as weeds.

(2) His last task that day, chopping firewood for Mr. Brown, was great fun.

(3) David could not understand why the Cub-master, after a few more days of similar misfortunes, told him that he had done enough for the Pack!

(4) Was it his fault that the axe-head flew off and cracked Mr. Brown's shin?

(5) David Parks of the 28th Drystone Cub Pack always enjoyed the annual "Bob-a-Job" week and this year he was well prepared to earn hundreds of "bobs".

(6) Window cleaning was his next job.

(7) Weeding was his first task and a very easy one it was, thought David.

(8) What a pity that he accidentally shoved the ladder through those two windows!

ORAL COMPOSITION

Use your imagination and common sense to answer the questions below. Before answering, think out carefully what you are going to say. All your answers must be spoken in good, clear *sentences*. Remember, there can be more than one correct answer to these questions.

A. (1) How would you teach your young brother or sister to cross the road?
   (2) What would you do if you found a purse containing £5?
   (3) Which season of the year do you like best and why?
   (4) If you were lost in a strange town, what would you do?
   (5) Will you start smoking when you grow up? Give reasons for your answer.

B. (1) If someone gave you £5, what would you do with it?
   (2) Which animal do you prefer as a pet and why?
   (3) If you had the choice, would you prefer to live in a town or in the country? Give reasons for your answer.
   (4) Which is your favourite television programme and why?
   (5) If you had to make a long journey, would you prefer to travel by car, bus, train or plane? Give reasons for your answer.

Look at the pictures and then fill in the blank spaces in this little story:—

Bob and his sister, Mary, are .... to see the snow. When it has stopped snowing, out they go to .... a snowman. They work hard with their .... and, although it is ...., they soon feel warm. When they have finished, Bob puts his father's old .... on the snowman's head and a .... in his mouth. Mary uses stones for .... and puts a .... stick under the snowman's arm. Mother calls them in for .... The sun comes out and .... brightly. This makes the snow .... When the children .... to see their new friend, he is ruined.

Look at the pictures and then fill in the blank spaces in this little story:—

It is very hot in the .... The sun beats down, drying up the .... A bird, feeling very ...., suddenly comes across a jar which .... a little water. The mouth of the jar is ...., and he .... how his beak can reach the water. He is a clever bird and soon hits upon a good .... He collects .... and drops them, one by one, into the jar. The .... of the water rises, until, at ...., the bird is able to ....

Look at the pictures and then fill in the blank spaces in this little story:—

Rover steals a .... bone from the .... shop. On his way home he meets Grip, another big dog who is always very .... The two begin to fight and Rover .... the bone. The dogs move farther and farther .... from the bone. Scotty, a tiny dog who would be no .... for either in a fight, ... the bone and .... quickly with it, leaving the two .... still quarrelling, unaware that they are fighting over .... at all.

Look at the pictures and then fill in the blank spaces in this little story:—

This is Michael. He has been .... to take a bath — which he does not like to do. While he is filling the bath, he has an idea. Why not .... his hair slightly and then pretend that he has taken his ....? This he does, and waits for ten .... before leaving the bathroom.

"That was a .... bath," he says to his mother, who smiles at him. "I feel a lot ...."

"Oh, do you?" she says. "That's very strange because you forgot to take in a towel and soap with you. What did you wash yourself with, and how on earth did you manage to get ....?"

The little .... was trapped.

Study the following sets of pictures carefully. Answer the quest-ions by means of *well-formed sentences*. Your completed answers should make up a short composition or story.

Picture (1)
- *(a)* Who are in this picture?
- *(b)* What is the bird doing?
- *(c)* What is the cat doing?

Picture (2)
- *(a)* What is the boy doing?
- *(b)* Has the bird seen the cat?

Picture (3)
- *(a)* What is the cat doing now?
- *(b)* What has the boy picked up?
- *(c)* Do you think the stone will hit the bird?

Picture (4)
- *(a)* What has the stone done?
- *(b)* Did the cat get its dinner?
- *(c)* Do you think the boy did the right thing?

Picture (1)
    (a)   Who are in this picture?
    (b)   What are they doing?
    (c)   Are they in the city or in the country?
    (d)   What does the notice say?

Picture (2)
    (a)   What are the boys doing now?
    (b)   Does it look safe?
    (c)   Are they being foolish or wise?

Picture (3)
    (a)   What does this notice say?
    (b)   Is there anything else in the picture?
    (c)   What should the boys do here?

Picture (4)
    (a)   What has happened to the bicycles?
    (b)   What has happened to the boys?
    (c)   Where have they landed?
    (d)   Do you think they have hurt themselves?
    (e)   Do you think the cow is surprised?

In the following exercises you are asked to study carefully the pictures and the part of the story that is given. Your task is then to complete the story by explaining the remaining pictures in your own words.

Mr. Roberts, the postman, knocks at the door of No. 17. Mrs. Allen opens it. With her is her little daughter, Barbara, who is four years old today.

Look at the last two pictures and complete the story in your own words.

Tom is returning from school one afternoon. He sees smoke pouring from the downstairs window of a house in his street.

Look at the other pictures and complete the story in your own words.

Bob and Joan are enjoying a day at the sea-side. They build a lovely sand castle and decorate it with sand pies. Bob puts a flag at the top. Then Mother calls them to have sandwiches and tea.

Look at the last two pictures and complete the story in your own words.

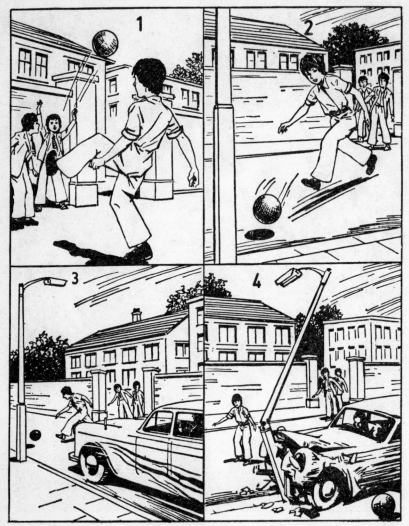

Bob is playing at football with Jim and Fred. He kicks the ball hard and it soars high over the wall into the roadway. Bob rushes through the gates to get it. He does not stop to look when he reaches the road.

Look at the last two pictures and complete the story in your own words.

Just look at Jack. What a naughty boy he is — scrambling over Farmer Grey's wall! And what is he doing now? He has climbed up a tree and is helping himself to some fine, ripe apples. But what is that? A bark?

Look at the last two pictures and complete the story in your own words.

The Carroll family is preparing to go on holiday. John and Margaret watch Mother finishing the packing. Mr. Carroll is putting on his coat.

"I think that is the sound of the taxi outside," he says.

Look at the other pictures and complete the story in your own words.

On the next few pages you will find a number of pictures of men and women, animals and things. Each picture is accompanied by questions for you to answer. If you answer each question *in a sentence* you should, when you have finished, have a short composition. Read this through and make sure that it makes complete sense and that you have not forgotten full stops and capital letters. The first is done for you as a model.

(1) What is the man in the picture?
(2) What does he do?
(3) How is he dressed?
(4) What is he holding in each of his hands?
(5) Where would we find him?

The man in the picture is a chef. His job is to cook meals for people. He is dressed all in white with a white apron and a tall, round, white cap. In his left hand he is holding a saucepan, in his right a fork. We would find him in the kitchen of a hotel or restaurant, or perhaps even on board ship.

(1) What is the lady in this picture?
(2) Where would we find her?
(3) What subject is she dealing with at the moment?
(4) What other subjects might she teach?
(5) Why must she be very, very patient?
(6) Why is her work so important?

(1) What is the man in this picture?
(2) What is he doing?
(3) What has he in his hands?
(4) Has he caught any fish?
(5) Is he fishing in the sea, in a lake or in a river?
(6) Why must he be very patient?
(7) Can you name any of the fish he might catch?

(1) What is the lady in this picture?
(2) Where would we find her?
(3) What does she use to fit the dresses?
(4) What "tools" does she use in her job?
(5) Name as many materials as you can which she might use.

(1)   What is the man in uniform?
(2)   What building is he guarding?
(3)   What jewels are kept there?
(4)   What has the sentry in his hand?
(5)   Do you think it is loaded?
(6)   Would you like his job?
(7)   What are the other people in the picture doing?

(1) What is the lady with the glass in this picture? _
(2) What is her main task?
(3) What do we call people who are ill?
(4) Where would you find this lady?
(5) Who else works there?
(6) Why is this work very important?

(1) What is the man in this picture?

(2) Why does he need very strong muscles?

(3) What does he use to cut down trees?

(4) What could he use instead?

(5) What is used to carry away the logs?

(6) What is used to load the logs?

(7) Are you a good detective? In what country do you think this takes place?

(1) What is the girl in this picture?
(2) What do you know of her job?
(3) Why must she have knowledge of several languages?
(4) Why must she be very cool-headed?
(5) Why must she be fond of children?
(6) How is she dressed?
(7) Would you like to do her work? Why?

(1) What is the man in this picture?
(2) What is he doing?
(3) What grips the wood while he is working on it?
(4) Can you name some of the other tools he uses?
(5) Can you name some of the articles he makes?
(6) What would you call the place where he works?
(7) What do you think would be scattered over the floor of such a place?

(1) What are the girls in this picture?
(2) Where would we see them?
(3) Why must they train so hard?
(4) Do they travel a great deal in their work?
(5) Who provides the music for them?
(6) Can you name any famous ballet in which they might dance?
(7) Would you like to do their work? Why?

(1) What is this animal?
(2) What colour is he?
(3) Is he a wild or a tame animal?
(4) In what part of the world does he live?
(5) Where would we find him in this country?
(6) What does he eat?

(1) What is this animal?
(2) Is it a wild or a tame animal?
(3) What does it eat?
(4) Who looks after it?
(5) What things do we get from it?

(1) What is this animal?
(2) What colour is it?
(3) Is it a large or a small animal?
(4) With what does it pick up its food?
(5) Do you know what its tusks are made of?
(6) In which parts of the world does it live?

(1) What is in this picture?
(2) What is the colour of its sails?
(3) What is at the top of its mast?
(4) How many people are on board?
(5) What is driving it through the sea?

(1) What is in this picture?
(2) What is it standing in?
(3) What are lighting it up?
(4) What is there at the very top?
(5) What are tied to its branches?
(6) Why are children so delighted to see it?

(1) What is in this picture?
(2) What are its colours?
(3) What is the colour of the light at the top of the beacons?
(4) What are the beacons for?
(5) Why should we always try to cross the road here?

You have been learning to write little stories about people, animals and things by answering questions about them with pictures to help you. Now see if you can write three or four sentences about each of the following. Make your little stories as interesting as you can.

A Policeman
A Sailor
A Postman
A Cobbler
A Pilot
A Hairdresser
A Shop-Girl
A Waitress
A Traffic Warden
A Camel
A Polar Bear
A Donkey
A Parrot
Traffic Lights
My Birthday Cake

STORIES TO BE COMPLETED

In each of the following exercises a composition has been started but not finished. By using your imagination complete each story in as interesting a way as you can. What you write should be about the same length as the part given.

Here is a model to guide you.

Desdemona was one of those patient little donkeys we see every summer on the beach. She was able to make friends with everyone — even with other animals. One day a travelling circus arrived at Sandcombe at the height of the holiday season. When Desdemona saw the cages of lions, tigers, monkeys and rare birds set up camp in the field next to where she grazed, she longed to join them ....

AND NOW HERE IS HOW IT COULD BE COMPLETED.

She trotted to a spot where the hedge was low, took a short run at it and leaped. Soon she was wandering freely among the cages and ropes and tent poles, but not for long. A boy, mistaking her for one of the performing animals, led her into the Big Top. Here she joined six ponies which were trotting round a ring and jumping over boxes. Desdemona tried to do the same but knocked everything down. The trainer, laughing, led her out and it was discovered that Desdemona was not part of the circus. After a short time, quite happy with her adventure, she was returned to her own field.

Now try the exercises which follow.

(1) Children are very fond of Desdemona because of her sweet temper and sad face. One day, however, she surprised them all. One of her customers, a little boy, clambered on to her back, yelling that the redskins were on the warpath as he kicked his heels into poor Desdemona's ribs and used her ears as reins. Donkeys are said to be stupid but Desdemona knew how she was going to put a stop to this. Her usually sad face seemed to smile as she headed for the water's edge ....

(2) Desdemona was very fond of sweets which she often received from Jill, her master's fifteen-year-old daughter. Jill had even taught her to beg like a dog by holding the sweet high in the air above her head.

Desdemona groaned one day when a very fat lady declared that she would like a photograph of herself sitting on a donkey. The poor animal's legs almost buckled as the lady was helped to mount. A gentleman in the crowd held up a sweet to make Desdemona raise her head as the photograph was being taken ....

(3) Desdemona sometimes wore an old, battered, straw hat which was pulled tightly over her long ears. One day a boy, unnoticed by Desdemona's master, stole the hat. All day long Desdemona watched the rascal paddling in the water.

Late in the afternoon a child wearing an old straw hat was heard shouting for help from a sandbank. It was the thief. The tide had cut him off and there he was, stranded and afraid. Before anyone could move, Desdemona splashed through the waves towards the boy ....

(4) Desdemona had a special friend among the children. This was Tommy who always brought her tasty carrots and lumps of sugar. One day, when business was slack, Tommy was given a ride for nothing. As the boy and donkey were alone, Desdemona decided that she would like a little gallop; and off she went ....

(5)   After her day's work was over, Desdemona was given a rub-down, a good feed of oats, a long drink of water and then turned loose in her field. Unknown to her master, some tinkers were camped in a nearby clump of trees. They watched Desdemona as she grazed in the field and during the night one of them led her off ....

(1)   Monica, for the eighth time that day, had been misbehaving. As a punishment, Mummy had removed her doll and placed it on a high shelf out of Monica's reach. The naughty child said she would stand on the table when everyone was busy but Mummy made her promise not to set a foot on any piece of furniture. Monica was true to her word but her eyes lit up when she saw the dozens of books in Daddy's book-case ....

(2)   One day Monica and I, wearing new dresses, set off on a picnic. Monica grumbled when I made her carry the basket and I could see that she was planning mischief. Soon we came to a barbed wire fence and before I could stop her, Monica darted through a narrow opening. When I tried to follow I ripped my dress; nor could I climb over. There was no way across for me and as I pleaded in vain for Monica to return to my side of the fence, she only grinned and started to unpack the basket ....

(3)   Daddy is a policeman and often lets us children play with his hat, truncheon and whistle. One day Monica found his handcuffs and key. We played at detectives and I foolishly let Monica handcuff my wrist to the towel rail.

"You *will* come back?" I shouted as she went in search of more robbers to arrest. Monica merely laughed ....

(4)   I had to take Monica to the hairdresser's. On the bus she seemed to be behaving herself and I sat back to read my magazine. At one of the stops the conductor went into a shop to deliver a parcel. Unknown to me, Monica reached up and pressed the bell. The bus moved off without a conductor ....

(1)   Billy Jenkins delivered newspapers every day after school. With the money he earned he was able to buy a set of new darts – something he had wanted for a long time. He was hurrying home with the box of darts in his pocket when he noticed two men park a motor cycle at the kerb and enter a jeweller's shop. Seconds later a shot was fired. *Robbers*! thought Billy. He looked at the motor cycle and pulled out his darts ....

(2)   Billy was in a hurry to finish his newspaper round before dashing off home. As he pushed a paper through old Mrs. Walker's letter-box he smelled gas. Billy rang the bell but there was no answer ....

(3)   Part of his paper round led Billy Jenkins past an old, ruined house which was supposed to be haunted. Most of the children in the area kept well clear of it at all times. One wintry day as Billy was delivering his evening papers, he saw a light through the trees. It came from one of the rooms of the haunted house ....

(4)   Billy sometimes borrowed his brother's racing bicycle for his paper round. One evening, when he had only one more paper to deliver, he heard a cry in the Main Street.

"Stop him! Stop him! He's stolen my purse!"

Billy looked up and saw a woman pointing to a boy of fourteen who was running like a hare along the pavement. Billy began to pedal very fast ....

(1)   For months Jim had been saving his pocket money every week and at last had enough to buy a little puppy from the pet shop at the corner. One afternoon he arrived home with his pet. There was only one snag. Mr. Brown knew nothing of the new member of the family and had even been heard to say that he did not like dogs. Jim decided that he would leave Spot in a basket upstairs till after Father had finished dinner. Mr. Brown was generally in a better mood after a good meal ....

(2)   Spot lay on the rug near the fire. The family had just left the dining-room and plates, cups, saucers, a bowl of fruit, milk jug and sugar bowl were still on the table. Spot rose to his feet wondering what mischief he could do. He sniffed round the table and found that he was just able to reach the corner of the tablecloth ....

(3)   One morning about eleven, Mrs. Brown came in from her morning shopping and laid the meat for the dinner on the kitchen table. She was unaware of Spot lying in his basket, eyeing her every movement. She then hurried to the front door and stood for a minute or two speaking to the laundryman who had called ....

(4)   When Spot was a little bigger, Jim taught him to carry a folded newspaper in his mouth. One morning, as Jim was leaving for school, he found a huge pile of newspapers on the front step — thirty-two to be exact. He remembered that the newspaper boy was a lazy rascal who did not bother to push the papers through the letterboxes but left them on the steps. At that moment Spot dashed through the gate with the thirty-third. What was Jim to do? ....

(1)   Jack's home was in a road which was very steep, and on his way to school he often used to hang on to the backs of heavy lorries as they crawled uphill in low gear. At the top, before they began to travel faster, he would jump off and find himself almost at the school gates. One afternoon, however, he tried his usual trick but, to his dismay, as he was about to jump off, he discovered that a red van was following close behind ....

(2)   One morning during the Easter holidays Alice was walking along High Street when she heard what sounded like pistol shots. Her eyes popped when three masked men hurried out of a bank, two gripping pistols, the third a bulging brief-case. They jumped into a waiting car which drove off with a roar. Alice dashed to a telephone box round the corner but in her haste she failed to notice some people grouped round TV cameras which were busy filming the scene ....

Printed by Martin's The Printers Ltd., Berwick upon Tweed